Dante's
Unintended
Flight

Other Books by Emily Vogel

First Words (NYQ Books)
Digressions on God (Main Street Rag Press)
West of Home (with Joe Weil) (Blast Press)
The Philosopher's Wife (Chester River Press)
Still Life with Man (Finishing Line Press)
Elucidation Through Darkness (Split Oak Press)
An Intimate Acquaintance (Pudding House Press)
Footnotes for a Love Letter (Foothills Press)

Dante's Unintended Flight

Emily Vogel

The New York Quarterly Foundation, Inc.
New York, New York

NYQ Books™ is an imprint of The New York Quarterly Foundation, Inc.

The New York Quarterly Foundation, Inc.
P. O. Box 2015
Old Chelsea Station
New York, NY 10113

www.nyq.org

First Edition

Set in New Baskerville

Layout by Raymond P. Hammond

Cover Design by Raymond P. Hammond

Cover Art: *Uncovered Man and Women,* ©1983, pencil, 20 x 30 in.
by Marco Muñoz Jaramillo | www.artphotomylove.blogspot.com

Author Photo by Joe Weil

Library of Congress Control Number: 2017931331

ISBN: 978-1-63045-046-5

Dante's
Unintended
Flight

Alla luce di attraversamenti di campo,
per il mio amore triade: Joe, Clare, e Gabriel.

There is a distance like the sky which binds us and makes us liable. You conjure your lineage and become big as a room, a morning twitch of brain or indecision. The muted world is trafficking outside like insects in the sun. An infant wails on the street and it is in any language and no language. It is the barbaric yawp of the transient world, the gut of it like sprawling water, for lack of conscience or transgression. Mere wailing, the cry of an unwitting air, a woman wandering alone and glad for her loneliness. Man is an epidemic, a greeting and a construct. It ambulates like a beautiful contagion. It is the anticipation of fire or something more grand and meaningless. After death perhaps is light without meaning. A star-spent and drifting void of the self. Small intervals of memory, exonerated from their mortal weight.

A child holds a spoon poised at her ear and begins a conversation. Her mother wants to close her eyes forever. Man is an involuntary twitch. An intention that aspires to set free the fathoms and caves of the mind. Woman dangles from his rib like a twig. She widens her legs and becomes the framework of a city. Soon the sinister and the presumably holy commence their histories. There are automobiles and electric brains. Hearts like sinking objects in the body or hearts as pervasive grievances that sing in solitary rooms. They sound very literal, like organs, or they sound very melodic like stories. There is no such thing as a heart and there is nothing without a heart.

There are strange exchanges with familiar people and familiar exchanges with strange people. Man is a translation of himself, in anger or congeniality. Man is a fixture among a sea of orbiting abstractions. Woman is something leafy which climbs a trellis and solemnly proceeds in its climbing. Woman sits silent and pregnant in the well beneath all language. Her interchange is with a whisper of air. An infant is a prayer and day becomes evening and evening becomes night and nobody says a word. In the late morning, laundry billows outside the shuttered window.

Sound mutilates with distances. Summer estranges the mind from its mind. Sometimes woman sits when she is alone and the mind attempts to find itself. The dream of existence is a distraction from the horror of existence. Or the beauty of existence is an unnoticed propagation. It is an occasional impact like the sunlight in the spaces between leaves. It blinds the woman like a drug and makes her delirious with an influx of language and despair. She fills her glass and sits as if she was a man. She thinks as a man thinks she is thinking. She thinks despite what a man thinks she is thinking. A jackhammer rages outside like a human devouring another human. And the human's mouth is vast with words that choke on their own rage.

A little boy is an entry into symbol and inherits himself as symbol. He becomes a situation like an availability of food and wine. He becomes a philosophy of numbers and knows himself as this. He sleeps and is for lack of condemnation that he will one day become man. Woman has allowed him to enter as symbol and then desires to eat him. She longs to swallow him again so that he is nothing, a seed that is imminent, and becomes itself, is swallowed, longs to become, enters, is swallowed. It is the entering and the swallowing which allows him to exist. The swallowing and the free-fall again into symbol, a weightless orbiting and ordering.

The coordinates of a voice are negotiable by the air which carries them. Woman hears a voice and it is in the mind or it is from the spaces of shuttered windows. The voice says, "Bella Bella," or the voice says, "Woman has stuffed her grievance into her dead soul and carried it with her like luggage." The voice cries into the Florentine afternoon and insists that she is a counterpart. And she recalls the ear of the voice which sounds like a man in the walls. A voice in the midnight walls like a guide against the incidental and random. Soil strewn on the terrace and kitchen floor, dismembered woman like imminent angel. God proceeds with his narrative and nobody has any idea.

Both the woman and her lack of voice are the sound of brooms sweeping on the street. She is the sweep of the street, the transit of rhapsodic humans. She is squelched by the voices and she blooms in her own absence of self. She is the bloom of things for lack of their bloom. She is no longer young but she is not the old woman in supermercado buying detergent and troubling over her change. And she is. She is old and troubling over her change. She is debris among the drifting debris. A crowding of humans in choreographed chaos, their voices rising like the fast birds of the Florentine sky. Her sex like an opaque window insisting that she swallow and be swallowed in an obliteration of all language. Her mind deep in the soil, among the roots of trees.

A little boy is at the threshold of the shuttered window at dawn, entranced as the morning birds. The morning birds traverse in a fast circling of calligraphic majesty. The mother's voice echoes from beyond the threshold of the shuttered window in variants of sound. The boy's father comes to the window, unmoved by the spectacle of birds and then dissolves into the apartment. He dissolves as though he is an afterthought and becomes an image in a vague chronology. The cinema of it is a preface to a small and humble epic. Now there only voices. The stark reality of it is gothic and bright. Man does not inherit a singular voice. He is soft and low and full of languor, measured, and with intervals of a contemplative hush, or he is the raucous boom of late morning. Seven a.m., and the heavy clang of Santa Croce bells are peeling, reeling the daylight into allocations of time.

The laughter of televisions rouse the sleeping city. Man is becoming something which circles his own center, dumbfounded and grief-stricken. It is his belief that he should long for something ancient and beautiful, because he is a perpetual history. Woman appropriates herself to be adorned in similitudes of womanhood. She becomes the essence of air and voice, of color flouncing against backdrops of the city. Her feet are attempting delicacy for the sake of man. Her eyes attempt light and emerge out of dark spaces like hell into heaven, or fire into something for lack of meaning. She aspires to be meaningless. She aspires to be a vision, like calligraphic birds, and becomes annihilated, and becomes whole, becomes entirely human, despite her drifting self. At the center, man and woman emerge and dissolve, vacillate between meaning and the lack of it. The piazza is still dim with inactivity. There is only the traffic lights among an inert and anxious air.

The city is the routine of wheels turning. The sound of the louder wheels rips the air like the invisible rift between woman and man. Woman walks along Borgo la Croce with a little girl, the street infested with the waves of a crowd. Man stands like a sentinel of newsprint. And the city is the gridding of newsprint. There is a market where woman browses, filling her satchel with vegetables and fruits. It is onerous on Borgo la Croce. The late morning sun opens the sweat glands and makes woman squint her eyes so that the city is a delirious blur. She knows that her delicate feet are walking but she is displaced from her own sex. Her feet are delicate in theory but are really the feet of a man. This makes her ashamed and sorry. She is walking in theory or she is not walking at all. She is the bulk of a body moving through space. She wants to drift like the calligraphic birds and their delicate brushstrokes, so that someone will later recall her delicate brow and not know her. She wants to be extraordinary, like the highest order of muses, lest she become nothing. She moves on or does not move on and her face feels heavy with sunlight. Her face feels heavy with her corporeal existence, like flesh that cannot hide itself. And she must go on in her own being. She must go on zig-zagging through the city dwellers like nothing with a body. The little girl looks around with curiosity and has not entered her sex. She is an intersection, sharp and vulnerable like all imminent revolutions.

Man is the essence of fear. He arose from dirt and was afraid
of his displacement from the sky. He was afraid of his own
gravity and afraid of the internal organs housed by his flesh.
He was afraid of being a singular creature. Man is woman,
the throbbing heart that birthed her and made her distinct.
Now he is afraid of his distinction from her. He is afraid and
wants to build her back into him. Woman wants to inherit
man as an internal organ. She wants to eat and absorb him.
She wants to speak to him but the language does not suffice.
Woman regards the pigeons and the pigeons are from heaven.
A writing utensil is from heaven. A tomato is from heaven.
Genitals are from heaven and the intrinsic numbering of
the universe is from heaven. Little boy's attempt at words
is from heaven and hell is from heaven. Man descends and
feels heavy like water or chains. He cries, "Santa Maria, Santa
Maria," and his soul is clanging inside of him like rage, or
like Santa Croce at noon.

Woman is rendered mad but it is not because she slips like the daylight out from the front door. It is because she slips like the night and prowls the city streets like a loud wheel ripping the air. Like the dissociative mind of motorcycles or the fast burgeoning of the world's anger. The world of the man-machine deters even the most beautiful of women. She is kin to the wild moon, to the wild river. It makes her animal and confused amid an unfamiliar landscape of small sound, of gigabytes and incremental nonsense. Music is scarce or exploited. Music is on channel seven in Florence, singing, "Oh Maria…"

The priests are soft spoken but they are not woman. They are not overcome by their own wombs. They are harbingers of reason and the reasonable order of things. Little boy lies sleeping like a carnival after two a.m. Little girl opens the previously closed door and wanders out into the heavy sunlight. "Ave Maria…Ave Maria…" the six p.m. rosary summons the cooler winds of the early July dusk. And one man is sleeping in the clean laundry. He is man and woman and scales the midnight streets singing "Ave Maria" to a homeless and greater God. Homeless God drinks the air and is not lonely. Homeless God is stuck in the loud wheel. Homeless God is initiating rain where there is no rain and heavy sun where saints can withstand it. Saints disappear into cloisters and sit in the dark and disremember their own corporeal forms. They disremember their genitals and swell like souls, in complete annihilation of themselves. In this is a thin air that sings. In this is the tentative string of thought, trailing off into the dream of death and all that follows, fast angels darting between here and nowhere.

Woman is sometimes a representation of herself. She is the span of a city street in the late morning, and she is child, banging on a glass door as if to be let inside from a December snow. She is Ligozzi's tiny flowers, their wiry roots extending and spiraling into blank space. She is embraced by the great arm of an illustration of God, or she is adorned in a long gown with Bambino Christe cradled in her lap, his tiny penis like a severed thumb. Christ among the chaos, Christ the son of man, Christ and his pronounced ribcage offering mercy out of destitution. Destitution is the inside of a rock where nothing lives and the darkness sings its empty fathoms so that nothing is singing at all. It is the orchestra of the mind, the voice of the mind which instructs the voice of the mouth to utter language.

Man is an ancient and massive head that is eventually carved into stone. Woman is an ancient and massive head that throttles a swan and calls it triumph or calls it defeat. She brings the fruit and the serving plate, and a temperate and perfumed air. Fire made man and man brought fire to man and fire condemned him to stone. Man is stone or man is destitution or man is serving me sausage and wine. Man is three o'clock, or man is eight o'clock, or man is the day turning into night, turning into the unrelenting procession of time. And time is a herd of cattle, proceeding together in a straight line until they are led to blood and slaughter. The fields are vast there when they are finally gone, a wasteland to proffer the divinity of seed, or man, wolf, man and his mighty staff. Man stands upright like a building made of stone and feels his heart like the city's pulse and feels his heart like a wasteland, the cattle grazing like ghosts.

Woman wants to be beholden and does not want to be beholden. She wants to putter and prepare for ecstatic things and does not want to putter and prepare. She wants to swallow a man and she wants a man to reign over a city. She does not prefer tomatoes but she enjoys eating them. Woman feels like a hairline crack in an egg. She feels like gullies that break over fields after the rain. She feels designated and appointed. She wants to remain designated so that she does not feel her body is careening from a high roof. Woman's pores open like sex when man is frying tomatoes and meat and when he inherits a type of omniscience. Woman feels God like a heavy air through the pores in the ceiling and the pores in the ceiling open to divine love. And love is nothing. Love is a word that is small as stray ash and disintegrates before love is completely there. Love calcifies the bones and makes them feel like dirty water. Little girl puts a shoe and a wedge of cheese into a bucket of dirty water and that is love. That is one quick bird in the Florentine sky.

There is a thin air which extends between the brain of a woman and the brain of a man that trembles like a vibration of sound. It is Ligozzi's hairline roots which curl and trail into blank space. In the blank space is conflict, a door left open or closed, a child removing her shoe in supermercado. The friendly cashier put the shoe back on and exclaimed, "Bravisimo!" In the blank space is a word spelled out slowly and with deliberation. It is the language of man gone lost to the sea where woman goes for refuge. Her alphabet keeps her alive. And the Florentine streets are alive with the ecstatic voices of a dim and languorous dusk. And the bells of bicycles ring like evening visitations, and an old woman comes to the window and opens wide the green shutters. Widows lament and rejoice. Widows fry tomatoes and weep for the ecstasy of living and the oncoming fear of death. The wind might rattle the dishes and their bodies are accumulations of desperate prayers. They feel peace like the dusk, like the God that is an ecstatic and beautiful nothing.

The birds are circling like the wayward ash that floats above a dead fire. The birds are the dead newspapers burning. Woman is a blade, an accommodation to herself. She brews coffee like a glad duty, is dog-like and deliberate. If you look at her face it is on the verge of shriveling inward from fear. She is God's second ministry or she is God's aesthetic flesh. She is on the street outside of Santa Croce losing her hair. She is on the street outside of Santa Croce counting her coins and singing. She is spinster or she is slave, a diurnal politic of herself. She is not rooted in the self; she is Ligozzi where the art was left blank. She is the danger of city traffic and she is in danger of city traffic. Man regards the small flower of the art, and little boy regards mother, and they are the same, little boy and man, and faith in the faith of breast and depiction, faith in the underworld of woman and approximation, faith in lily tucked behind the delicacy of an ear. Woman pours the milk for little boy, sips the coffee that was likewise brewed by woman.

Man is gun and man bludgeons woman and man bludgeons himself. A gun bludgeons itself for being a gun. Man envisions himself laid out in the rain-drenched street like sacrifice or defeat. Man wants not to be man, does not want his soul to inherit his captive body. Man wants to be a sarcophagus, deep as stone. Man envisions his own death and it is like pavement or the vibrancy of bluebirds. Man wants to be a window open to the illness of the cool afternoon. It begins to rain and the rain sounds like a bad telephone connection on the overhang. Woman wants her voice to be a clear bell like an articulation of love, her sex speaking in the comprehensive language of man. Her sex-like words, like blades, like bells, like the certainty of touching skin. Her sex wanting the hands of man gentle above her tailbone. Man or black fly, fatigue of living. The framework and ridicule of the polis, the history of useless books. The heart is not the distillation of theory. An image on a screen and a despairing gun, left lying on the unmade bed. Man, or despair, the dramatic nonsense of the polis. To justify existence, the polis makes its plans and constructs the groundwork, the earth and sea sustaining regardless.

Little girl is washing a plate, a knife, a chain, a towel, a padlock. She is washing these things and assigning them purpose and assigning purpose to herself. She has no need to feel anything less than purpose. If she feels no purpose it is of no existential concern. She'll stand in the sunlight and squint her eyes as the noise resounds from beyond the shuttered windows. Noise of mid-afternoon meal while little girl revels in the onerous sun. Man inherits the lack of purpose in manhood and tears at a hunk of bread. He feels purpose in bread and in ambulation. He feels no purpose in ambulation and he feels animosity from God. He feels God like bread and longs to eat him, feel God absorbed in his own gut. God is purpose and God is the lack of purpose. Man loves God and feels nothing reciprocal, like spitting into the river. Man wants to spit into the river and move on, under the presumption of the sky.

Duomo is the presumption of the sky and the sky does not
exist. There is no digital language here but the music in
the piazza is a distant and idyllic home. Tourists look on as
woman is outside the church losing her hair and counting
coins, and her heart swells into the city air, which is alive with
ambulatory man and woman, camera, wine, soft conversation,
and polizia sirens. Polizia sirens in the silent desert that once
was. Polizia sirens despite the noise of a distant America. And
America is frantic and dead, spinning like a wash cycle on
overload. And America retains its rock and roll and folk guitar.
And the wind is an element of vague faith in the romance
of God. Man asks questions but he is thinking of bigger
questions. Man is eating his fish with a very noticeable
nervousness. Man tilts his head to the air, thick with song
and lack of violence, and calls forth the muse, and does not
call forth the muse. He eats his fish and drinks his whiskey.
Woman interlaces her fingers, presses them to her lips,
and feels the essence of time like a mockery of itself. Later
woman feels a small death after relinquishing her sex to
man. The ceiling looks promising and warm and her eyes
are exhausted of their own sight. Woman wants to dissolve
into the nothing of darkness and forget. She wants to render
temporary things prolonged and does not. And she feels the
dull conflict of wanting to be nothing and wanting to return
to the eventual daylight.

Man is intricate mechanism. He is an elaboration of muscular language and cock. In the hot sun his face is talking but woman's ears are blurred by the ambient sound of voices. Her sex is the winding streets of the city, where they curl and narrow into the pin-dark of incidental shadow. Her sex is open wide as the piazza where woman and bambino pass, where men's accordions breathe a delirious sound in the sun. Woman feels she will become cobblestone, her body will tire and become stone simply because it is tired of being a body. If she is not a body then she is the evening sky. If she is not a body then she is the eye of God seen through the eye of God. It is Sunday and a madness of church bells clang in the air. The bells are wild like the ghosts of the ancient and holy tearing through the city in flamboyant costume, the colors flying everywhere like drunk spectacles. Meanwhile the electric world propagates and the endless clicking of digits proceeds in its climbing toward some myth of heaven. Soon they will bust the sky and drown in air. Soon they will disintegrate and there will only be earth and sea, woman and man roaming as if misguided and bewildered, exiled from the first garden and the last.

At dusk, the white towels that hang on the line outside of
the shuttered window are the woman's mind. The woman's
mind is unhindered as the white towels at dusk. Suddenly
there is a cacophony of dogs barking, which sound very
much like the mind of the man. Little girl goes to the yellow
window and dreams into them, like the sea. The sound
of a drill in the distance is the sound of man. Man in the
distance can be heard saying, "Sorry; kiss." Little girl offers
a cooking pot to her mother and wanders around placing
things where they are meant to go or not meant to go.
Where are things meant to go? Things are meant to go in
the designated places of houses which were devised by man.
Woman puts things in their designated places and swallows
a glass of wine. She imagines the glass falling and crashing
to the ground and the glass does not crash to the ground.
And the glass crashes to the ground but it is merely in the
mind. The mind crashing, little girl entering language as
though language were a house devised by man. Words in
their designated places on the tongue. Words streaming
through the adaptive mind and awkward on the tongue.
Polizia sirens like light in the falling dusk where the light
cannot be seen. The sound outside the mind which invades
the mind. The sound inside the mind which man does not
know. Little girl places the cooking pot among a bed of
flowers and says, "This."

Woman is a dragon-beast and her head is full of expanding flames. She strokes little girl's hair and little girl knows that her mother is a dragon-beast. Little girl approaches woman in the dark and leans against her leg. She brings a watering pail to its designated place. Little girl is woman in retrospect. She is the sleep of truth, rattling watering pails against the railing, attempting to crawl into a pail full of dirty water. She says, "Boom, boom, uh-oh," and the night is as dark as the mind of woman which is glowing white with language. Man is inside the house, glad for the things in their designated places and also unconcerned with their designations. Little girl cries in the dark, and woman estranges herself from words and their darkness. Words dissolve and become designated like places. Little girl brings the watering pail to woman and it is damp against woman's leg. Little girl gets lost in the dark and says, "boom." And the war of men continues regardless, in ambush, in silent distress, loud as woman's mind.

The fast birds in the Florentine afternoon appear as if they are shot one by one out of the sky. They drop and pivot behind the trees. The wall washers are washing the walls, the rough scraping like a solitary noise. Man has been chopping and cooking tomatoes and the aroma makes little girl and little boy softly snore in their sleep. Woman decides that tomatoes are of the essence, their robust perfume thick in the summer air. The birds rise again, as if resurrected from their tiny deaths. They rise and soar in arbitrary patterns. Woman recalls sitting by the sea and looking upward and upward, both aware and ignorant of her own futurity. The dragon-beast roar of airplanes pass overhead and it reminds her of this, of being little girl held captive by time. It is good to be held captive by time, if time is held captive by itself, and is "as it was in the beginning, is now, and ever shall be." There is no time, but circumstance which inherits the illusion of time. Man has always been in this place, chopping and cooking tomatoes. He is chopping and cooking tomatoes like an anticipation of his own ghost. After death, he will be chopping and cooking tomatoes.

Woman is always a preparation. While she is sweeping the floor, she is preparing for her vague futurity. The debris is stubborn, can never be entirely swept off of the floor. Some of it always remains, tiny particles of food or dust. The particles of dust could be the elements of her past that she struggles to annihilate. The past is an annihilation or man standing at the picture window waiting for the past to begin again. Woman is carrying bags full of food to man. The past and future are food and particles and shit. The past and the future are Sunday, again and again. Woman stands at the storefront window looking longingly at expensive shoes. The sun reflects off the window like an endless Sunday. And Sunday ends, again and again. And it is nevertheless eternally Sunday. Man is washing the walls, and little girl is in the dark bedroom, making flowers out of shit. Little boy is dreaming breast, rabbit, noise from a television, first memory of star, the eye adjusting to the blind light.

Man is making replicas out of beautiful things and woman
is making replicas of his replicas. Woman is reflected
in man and woman is man reflected. Woman imagines
the grumma-grumma of toads somewhere that is not the
city. She goes to retrieve medicines. She must tend to the
bleeding hands of man. Blood is letting from man's hands
and the blood is an eternal grief. Man must be liable for
the world and the world must be liable for him. Woman
must bear this liability. Man is the cry beyond the shuttered
window and woman must apply the salve. And the blood of
man's grief must be the world's liability. And woman must
mop the dirty floor and think of man as if man was drifting
astray in water, in blood, as he dreams of the drifting sky
while he lies supine in a dark room. Little boy sleeps, and
little girl is frightened by water, by blood. Man does not
know why he is destined to be man or ghost. Man does not
know why blood is the result of his liability. Man is blood
and woman weeps into him. Tears coalesce into blood and
man and woman are one body, one flesh, Christlike, a replica
in some museum on a hot afternoon.

Motorcycles are lined along the street like men, like an army, like an organized construct. Woman and little girl walk along the street with umbrellas and purses, stop and look at the cookware in the storefront window. They are as free as space between time's allocations and delighted as the lack of rain. Woman decides that the grumma-grumma of toads is the essence of living. It is man and woman, catching insects on their tongue like words. Words are insects and they fly around in variations of Italian dialect. Man is standing in the doorway and says, "Tres." Woman sips a glass of wine and swivels her hips. When she asks for food or bags she says, "Tres." She thinks trinity. She thinks magic circle, earth, air, sea. Man tears at a panini and swallows hard. The grumma-grumma of toads is the house of the mind, in a place that is the opposite of city. And man and woman are always among the grumma-grumma of toads. The grumma-grumma is the well beneath all language and is superior to language. Woman rides her bicycle with bambino on the back. Borgo la Croce is a lovely choreography of man and woman, and the afternoon is not pin-dust or pin-dark. Man gruffly says, "Bonjourno," and woman walks on, despite her aching feet.

Yesterday evening woman sat and looked at the sky and loved man. She loved man for being needed as though he were a relentless chase. Woman wanted to be infused by the city, by man and woman in rivalry or communion, all sitting in outdoor cafes, sipping wine and blowing smoke into the air. Man passes by and offers the pleasure of smoke. Man stands rejected in a doorway and woman loves him for tumbling pitifully in the opposite direction. Woman is knife because she is a creature of compensation. Her eyes are knives because she has the instinct to survive in the building infested world. Not the infestation of man but the infestation of man's construction. It is beautiful and superfluous, euro exchanged in fast flashes. It is beautiful like buses circulating the city in a pure mathematical pattern. Little girl raises her arms and praises the wall. What does she love? A wall built by man, a woman's knee. She rests her head on woman's knee amid the chaos of the digital world.

Woman is worthy only insofar as man determines her worth.
Man is sentinel and Eros or he is the soil out of which the
red geraniums blossom. Woman stares at the red geraniums
and does not see them. They look red and delicate but the
woman only sees the inside of her mind which is swarming
with visions of man as sentinel and as Eros. Man is transaction
and woman is transaction. Woman is menses red as the red
geraniums and red as the blood which pours forth from the
hands of man. And man and woman are the blood of stars
to which the tourists raise their heads and exclaim that this
is the most spectacular night of their lives. And every night
is the most spectacular night swarming with stars, the heart
absent, the eyes agents of delusion and illusion. God keeps
the incessant traffic in transit, and man keeps God above the
incessant traffic, weeping, beasts and dragon-beasts swarming
the city in bars and in amphitheaters, in the heat of drunk
air and seduction, the red geraniums starkly red against the
unclouded sky. Among this woman feels the sway of the city:
polizia sirens, the voices of woman and bambino, the watery
light on the trees.

There is watery light in the blur of man passing by on a bicycle and there is watery light all through Duomo. The horse drawn carriages are passing in a blur of watery light, their hooves clattering on the cobblestone. Woman sits alone and enjoys her meal as though she were a Russian novelist's muse or as though she was searching for a muse. Man arrives and arrives, offers her water and wine, coffee and liquor. Woman is in the mind of muse and muse is a blur of watery light. Woman's mind is the blank of watery light. She is pleasure in the afternoon. She is woman, little girl, drifting geranium in the wind. She drifts into stores, restaurants, museums, like the thought of woman or man drifting in vicissitudes among the piazza. Man is an illness in the blur of watery light. Woman is any number of lilies in Monet's watery light. Woman enters a dark room and observes the radical color in Pollack's paintings. It is dark and the music is ominous. America is the place of absence except where it is resurrected in watery light. Pollack puts on his work boots and watches his brain scatter on the canvas. In the center of Duomo, the horses are sleeping. The horses are sleeping a dead sleep in the midst of it, and horse is man, and horse loves man, and the wild piazza is the dream that the sleeping horse is dreaming.

Voices rupture the morning air. Outside the shuttered windows, laundry hangs willowy and dying from the line. The traffic in Florence is always there, even when it isn't. Birds are small ruptures in the morning air. Woman is comprised of language, it comprises her biology and her sex. She watches the birds and senses something without linearity. Little boy lies on the floor, squealing at the ceiling. The sound of buses briefly rupture the morning air. And the birds, violently flapping their wings. Seven o'clock mass commences and the bells of Santa Croce rupture this lapse of morning. And the sunlight ruptures the sky, calls the mind into waking. Man whistles beyond the shuttered window, and the man is morning itself, encapsulating the city.

Man is Jew or man is Gentile; man is exchanging euro
on the street with man. Woman is bending down to greet
bambino in another language, which is any language and
the well beneath all language, which is intonations of
glee. Man greets woman and her face becomes the sun-
light, which is man reflected, the city reflected in woman's
mouth. Woman's mouth devours the city and she feels full
of her own sex. She feels beautiful and dangerous in the
vicinity of the voice of man. She steps onto the cobblestone
like a great dragon-beast, elephant, not panting, or fleeing,
or in the distress of woman. Man is leisure in the afternoon
and kneels to pray at woman's knee. And kneels to kiss the
knee of woman. He is driven by European humility. He is
driven to an unlikely kindness, to defy visions of man, of
infestations of architecture. Outside the shuttered window,
woman beats a dirty rug against the wall, and dissolves again
into the apartment.

Little girl negotiates little spoon and language. Little boy gurgles in a distant room. Man is Kafka or Chekov, dog yowls or man yowls, or woman is strolling along the cobblestone like a ghost of herself. Lilacs or grapes pervade a nearby tree. It is too arduous to discern the difference and not necessary to discern the difference. Man sounds like the replica of a superhero from beyond the shuttered window. Water is running and gardens are reluctantly and sadly blooming. A white sheet hangs morbidly from outside the shuttered window. Something is shifting or being built: a family, some produce truck, some plates leftover from lunch, a café with outdoor seating. Outdoors, man and woman sip café or de la birra, crostini and frommagio. Woman buys latte for little girl, bambino craning her neck into the sunlight, her eyes wide at the spectacle of the world, God in her blood where she is oblivious and glad.

God is breathing in the trees like a constant lung. The sky drifts like the slow drag of a city. Little girl is perplexed at the sight of a dead flower and deliberates. What should she do with the dead flower? What should she do with padlock and chain? Man cries, "Mangere!" from beyond the shuttered window and pots and pans clash and clatter. Little girl says, "Boom" and her face is the wide sunlight. There are no fast birds in the air, but a white sheet which has drifted astray into the branches of a leafless tree. The tree is the cryptic writing against the wall of the building, and the writing says nothing. And the writing says God. The white sheet has drifted into God's breath and the breath of a cryptic language. And the white sheet is caught motionless in the held breath of God. It is the time of prensare and man and woman are comprised in God's held breath and the day is held tight like a leaf. Little girl puts a pot-lid into a pail of dirty water and the wind begins, God just exhaling.

Woman feels the great beast of the world economy eating at her ear. Woman feels the endless frenzy of diurnal occupations eating at her ear. Woman feels glad and in oblivion when she stares at the geometric shapes of buildings in the gray night. Woman dances in the parlor and feels generations pulsing within her. Man wanders into Sante Croce and gives up his sanity to God. He feels the blood of Christ coursing from the walls. He feels the light of Christ all around his skin and in his maladroit dedication to his own manhood. He is an orange grove in Fort Lauderdale, Florida. He is wandering in an orange grove and sanity is of no immediate concern. And Christ is in the orange grove like a yellow apparition, wandering in the sun. And Christ is all orange and haloed. And Mary is walking crowned with the twelve stars which define her only womanhood. And Mary is woman, symbol and suffering, thin line walked unto death with merely one purpose. One purpose is woman and woman must die in fulfillment of that purpose.

Why should woman commit herself to the drudgery of mathematics? Mary said God equals bambino equals salvation, and the light came streaming from the stone-walled window, angel hovering from above. And Mary said yes and that was her solitary purpose. Vessel of purpose and girl in bar watching the scenery and sipping her house wine. Girl skirting the pavement in fashionable skirt with eyes like daggers for woman or man. Woman or Mary in modern landscape confused and shaken by the world's economy of things and exchanges. Little girl looks up in submission at woman's eyes and wonders and resents why she will one day be woman. She arranges objects in artistic patterns and claps her hands. And woman feels her heart like stone sinking into the dance of little girl and woman. And woman drifts like the drunk trees into the blind night and feels guilt in her skin. And woman feels man like there is a centipede growing between them, full of passion and estrangement, his walking shoes pounding the pavement with the faith of something greater than the sun, or something even greater than that greatness.

Woman feels the beast of another woman like a gorilla on her back. The woman is the embodiment of the modern world and she is pervading the city. She is snaking the city streets in tight pants and speaking in melodic inflections. Woman feels nothing when she feels the space between tree and building. Woman wants to take man into the house of her body and teach him things about his own constructs. Woman wants to take man to the top of a building and teach him how to jump off without jumping off. And woman wants to teach man about the late night delirium of sex where he is nevertheless welcome, in holes, in woman valleys and rifts, in the open doors of all love which prospers despite the world's economy. And woman wants to make man humble and tame, like fishing into the river on a late July afternoon. Walk on the beach or to check into a random hotel, woman merely a crossfade in the scope of narrative or flight.

Woman feels the contingency of her own absence. She is absent from her own reflection in man and absent from her own actuality. She is body and hunger at the lunch hour and the hunger mitigates her sense of being absent. Her mind is a reflection of the dome of sky and her mind determines the actuality of her body. Her mind is man and her body makes her mind less than man. Because of her body she is peripheral and lovely. She drifts alongside man and selects her words and phrases. She is woman in corset or woman in work boots but she is brain and hole, and contour and mouth. Mouth is entry and exit and mouth is the expelling of dirt. There is no air which leaves her and there is air encapsulating her shadowy form. Woman is shadow of man and man is expelled from her. Man is an expelling. Man is an expelling and a towering. Man towers and woman cannot withstand the towering so woman wears work boots. Or woman stuffs herself into and stuffs into herself and sits politely like a plant. Little girl feels her own captivity, repeats her mother when her mother says, "No." "No, no," she says and cowers into the corner of the room. Busts like a flower. Little girl is woman and woman is the corner of the room. Woman steps into the spotlight and is vulnerable and is a tower of stone.

Bicycles move along in necessary paths. Woman stampedes
the cobblestone amid the delirium of afternoon noise.
Man is occupied by things of the earth and the bread that
sustains him. Woman kneads the bread and dreams of a
previous century. Now is a previous century. The sun weighs
heavy on the air and there is no century. Woman arose from
sleep and felt the ending of things in the attenuated air of
morning. Woman arose from sleep and felt the afternoon in
a cruel undoing. A procession of things, end to beginning,
to the absence of self in the afternoon. To the dictations of
the mind and anger. To anger like a fast bird, dissolving into
the pin-dark of itself at a great height. There is no fiction
and there is fiction. There is the reconciling of an oblique
world in fiction. There is woman with empty gut and there
is woman with gut full of itself or child. There is Mary
stampeding the cobblestone amid the delirium of afternoon
noise. Sante Croce church bells are distant and resolute,
attune the ear to God or a city. Woman prepares the meal
and the conscience of the self, and the conscience is a long
distillation into dusk.

Woman looks at the way the shadow intersects with the sunlight on the dead palm tree. It ticks like a clock, shadow slicing the sunlight where time is housed in abstractions. The afternoon swells like an abscess, bloats itself in its own light and delirium. The nervous petals of the geranium flower stand bravely in the wind. From beyond the shuttered window a ball can be heard bouncing against the floor in a steady rhythm. Woman is flight but does not move. She sits motionless among a Kingdom of man's language, negotiating its music. Man slips in and out of rooms, cultivating his Kingdom of language. He fills a milk-bottle for little boy and quells his weeping. He fills a whiskey bottle for himself and quells his own weeping. Man is little boy and little boy sits unarmed against the world. Man against man, man for himself, man for woman, and man of woman. Little boy of woman. Boy and woman were once conjoined as one. Boy became boy when he encountered air and man. Man once encountered air after dwelling within woman and has a vague and fragmented memory of this. Man's life is a blink and he dwells in woman and returns to God, where Mary welcomes him into her unconditional arms, the sound of doves sustaining in the otherwise silent nowhere.

Woman anticipates the blight of America and becomes an insect. Her mind becomes an insect and also a wide sunlit field. Little girl and little boy frolic in the field. They are sexless and superior to language. They are the well beneath all language, oblivious to their biology. Woman anticipates the blight of America and out in the street polizia sirens sound like dying beasts. This is the dying beast of transit from Italy to America. Wailing in the air, little boy wailing from beyond the shuttered window, wailing the wash cycle and the silent wail in the sheets hung on the line. The wail of trees, sustaining in their own histories. The history of trees superior to all language and the grumma-grumma of toads in the memory of trees. The quiet refuge by the pond, woman not man and man not woman, and woman not woman. Man a simple refuge of himself, undaunted by the Kingdom of his own language. Man impervious to his own constructs among the grumma-grumma of toads. He buries his head in woman's lap and remembers dwelling within her. He remembers the house of woman like a fever of wind, all infestations of buildings dissolved into the distant city. He is beside the pond, surrounded by the grumma-grumma of toads, and he is without time, and he is the eternal nothing that dwells inside woman.

Woman dreams at night of the self, projected, and dies. The rooms are dark like a slow dawn. People are asking questions as to where they find woman's things so as to remember her by. There is a quiet fountain running in the hallway. But woman is not woman. Woman is the self that she longs to be and man is touching her cheek. In sleep woman feels that she would rather be less than man. In dreams man is a memory without reason. He is a random memory of nothing important in memory. It is a memory of man staring into the bright light of some oblivion. Of hallucinating bright light while staring into bright light. Woman remembers Santa Croce like the way she remembers something that did not occur. Like something envisioned in America ringing nowhere and calling the morning air into the day's slow trajectory. Woman stands on the landing and watches the birds and the birds are nothing and the birds are the mind which traces the memory of the self, in dreams or in the mind of man. There is immanence here which is dormant and morose. She watches the birds cut through the fog and tries to fathom why she is body standing in the actuality of non-dream. She is non-dream and in waking she is a rude apparition. Man is eternally awake and occupying rooms like a differential. Little girl sleeps and dreams and does not know what a dream is.

Man is making love to the projected self of woman. She is leg, breast, shoulder blade, closed eye. Woman is the illusion of herself. She is not actual. Her eyes are closed and she is the dark sky in which the stars are ensconced. She is not biology. She swarms like the dark sky. Man is the earth and feels estranged from all pursuant afterlives. He dreams of the afterlife and feels estranged. Woman is already afterlife. Woman is afterlife prior to her own birth. Little girl does not that she has been born and little boy does not know that he has been born. They know mouth, hand, the tactility of thing. The know foot and purpose and the responsibility of foot. They know here and there like a distance that makes them weep. Intention is born in bambino and man. They do not swarm. Little girl sleeps and dreams of swarming but does not swarm when she wakes. She dwells between here and there and intends only ambulation. She intends language and curates sound. Her sound is directed at air. At man and at woman who are bodies in air. Differentials and intonation. Little girl and little boy do not know biology but they know intonation
and the way the body fills space.

When woman enters language, she has no face. How could that differential of purple flowers be blooming on the lilac bush? The lilacs are brown and dead and dry as brains. Beside them soft flowers bloom. Language is the soft flowers and woman stands before them with no face. She is aware of her upright body and begins to enter actuality. But nothing is actual. She vacillates between actuality and illusion. Man enters and renders her actual and does not see her actuality. He does not see the dead lilacs which are dry as brains. Woman's brain is not a dead lilac. Woman's brain is the soft flowers blooming and man is fascinated with the soft flowers but does not see them. Man sees woman's brain like the dark sky in which the stars are ensconced. At night he dreams and is not aware. He wakes aware of his actual body. He wakes, and is aware vaguely of the soft flowers. Little girl wakes and tosses things onto the floor. The things are soft flowers and their differentials. They are not dry as brains. They are the language into which she begins to enter.

Black flies circle the garbage pails and America is abeyant amid its summer languor. There is a buzz in the air beyond the black flies and the birds sound like a drugged mind. America is neatly cornered and the trees labor at being trees. Woman is an irritation, a fleshy mass. Man is tending to the garden, his big man-hands comingling with the dirt. And his hands are dirt and the dirt is the blood of God. Man is a filter or a sieve, God's blood between his fingers. Man is boxy and slave. His ego is an egg. Woman cooks him eggs and beans in the morning and man revels in the feast. Woman is feast. Woman is a fat feast and never believes that she is beautiful. Woman's ego is her own loins which swell with a lunar ecstasy. Woman is lunar and moon and lost like the self in the dark sky in which the stars are ensconced. And the moon is lost like the night, swelling and dissolving. Like Sisyphus it never stops and never stops. The moon is exhausting, and woman resents the moon and woman is contingent upon the moon and woman is nothing without the moon. Man gets lost in the sun, like Christ, as he rises.

The hum of dusk elucidates the mind of woman. Woman
is in the church pew, singing off-key, or woman is flattering
man who kneels off-key and out of context. Woman ingra-
tiates herself to woman. Is it a scandal to stuff a five dollar
bill into your shoe during mass? To stuff it underneath your
bra strap? "Weeds," the priest says, "grow in the good soil
and there is nothing to be done." Nothing in the existential
sense to be done aside from pissing in the river. Man pisses
into the river and feels the ubiquitous hum of God. Man
wanders through the weeds and thinks nothing religious
of them. They irritate his ankles. They make him think of
cigarettes and whiskey. They make him think of walking a
long road with a cold back and dirty hair. Is it a scandal to
wish the congregation would dissolve into pre-birth at mass?
To dissolve into the tumult of Biblical eras? To dissolve into
the spaces between the clouds? Woman closes her eyes and
imagines this. World that preempts genitals and disillusion
and illusion of woman or man. World that pulls the evil out
of weeds and lets the barren land be stripped like silence or
the first and last God. The air above the barren land sing-
ing. And no man or woman hears the singing and no man
or woman pulls the evil weeds to their final death. Woman
stands among congregation and sings and does not sound
at all like the air above the barren land. Woman feels dis-
placed among a hundred hands, palms raised to praise an
estranged God. God, the stranger, the better-than-woman,
the exalted gold tower that does not break and which keeps
both man and woman stupid and drifting among the forge,
constantly forward.

At the threshold of dusk, birds sustain their sounding.
Woman and sky are simultaneous. They are one face and
the face is intercepted by the face of the God and the faces
in consort are a murky river. Woman reads the newspaper
or stands at the threshold of dusk while wayward and illusory
visions of numbers drift through her mind and around it.
They float like intentions, grievances, abstractions of air, the
forgotten voices of air which remind her of green evenings
and give her comfort. When she closes her eyes she feels
the tumult that surrounds her. Little girl places a pot and a
wooden spoon in front of the screen door. This is America
and the summer dusk is a crowd of men's voices. The voices
of children swarming in the Doppler air. The sound of
desperate dogs, yoking the soul of all prior summers. Is that
a dead cat or a bicycle pump? It lies inert in the grass and
woman thinks of the irony of mortal conquests. Mortality
blooming like the soft flowers beside the dead lilacs, blooming
and then withering into their last green evening. Man walks
up and down the staircase like a scale on a lonely piano.
Man is a lonely piano or a diversion from the religion of
woman. Woman is leg, breast, shoulder blade, closed eye.
Woman is always closed eye, even in the brash and open eye
of daylight.

Woman is not solid. She traverses swiftly, pulsing forward like a river. She is nowhere but assumed actual and she is here. Her mind is a distant shore and she is taking out the garbage. Her mind is a distant shore and she is putting away the pots and pans. Her mind is a distant shore and man is there estranged from his earthly habits. He is wind and ghost, desperate dog of dusk. He is the threshold of dusk and has not assumed himself King of his construct. He is God's image in a prior place, slipping like a fish outside of his assumed construct and woman is pulsing forward. He houses himself in the pulse of woman, in the forward moving river. Neither man nor woman are anywhere. They are in the dream of God and not amid the construct of building-infested milieus. Everything is the dream of God and man and woman are not aware of their own existential stasis. There is no gridding of buildings. A small and modest house built by weeds. Personages passing like necessary mealtimes. The starving gut of existence now sublimated as a false longing. Plastic hip and lip, plastic breast and electric sex. Electric voice, faster than the necessary mind. Man and woman climbing up and up the infestation of buildings, falling unto their deaths and rising again like digits as constructs by way of the mind of man, which sustains itself in tyranny, or oppression.

Man is making love to woman like the mind of man. Moths remain inert against the side of the house underneath the porch lamp. Is it necessary for woman to always appear in her eternal youth? Gray hairs snake outward from the scalp and appear hoary. Woman and gray hair remain signified amid the construct of man and the infestation of buildings. Woman and gray hair remain a semiotic constraint. Man is ego and goes raging off into the lake. Woman is id and goes raging off into the lake. At the bottom of the lake they merge into nothing. They merge into the well beneath all language. They rise on a Sunday and bloom into the blur of lilies. It is the septic tank of America gone forgotten, Italy curling like articulate vines along a trellis, man and woman a forgotten imposition. It is the sadness which lives even prior to the rage into the lake. It is woman pulsing forward, her exhausted heart submitting to digits, the infestation of buildings. It is man, longing like a starving gut not for bread but for a slow passing on a Sunday. The threshold of dusk lives in the heart of man and becomes a cave. The threshold of dusk is a distraction to the infestation of buildings. Man remains quiet after the passing of dusk's threshold and remembers his own gut, the longing that kills him and also sustains him.

Woman contorts her face when she looks up at the sky. It is as incomprehensible to her as losing track of her own thoughts. She is in the house of her mind and the house is silent and the house is not a house. It is not a mind. Woman wanders purposefully through the garden and dissolves behind the trees. She dissolves like the house of her mind. Woman hears the voice of other woman and takes refuge behind the trees. The house of her mind is not the other woman's house, is not the other woman's mind. And their minds encircle each other in a great universal schema. And their minds are not the great immortal breast. There is immortal breast and the languor of man and woman in a dark room. And there is no time in the dark room. Whatever time there is might be transient and susceptible to annihilation. She leaves her hair unkempt. She spills tea on the pillow and carelessly mops it up, turns the pillow over, and falls asleep at three in the afternoon. She is always in the luxury of sleep. Sleep is the dead and she is ephemerally dead and in bliss. She dreams and wakes and eats. She revels in the body of a lover, feels the sleep in him like Eve. Their talk is fragmented, like the sound of various birds. Day is night, and night is day, and there is only the mere proximity of man and woman, circling each other like endless sex bereft of time. No construct but the body. Eventually woman sickens of this, awakens and orders man to chop the wood, tend to the garden, in which she feels as woman dissolved, and glad to be the dissolved nothing, the displacement of mind from body.

It has been resolved that the world is a garbage heap. It is the 21st century and man and woman are amongst a garbage heap, in a perpetual want for dominion. Woman becomes work-horse and drives for miles, negotiates the machinery of living. She negotiates the proper methods of dusting the corners in the ceiling. Little girl becomes fond of random objects and begins to arrange them. Begins to build and make sense out of seeming nonsense. Little girl wails for man and man drags his weary body in to sleep beside her. Little boy is sleeping in the luxury of a dark room. He is without time aside from the accumulation of garbage. He is without sex aside from the eventual entry into his own construct. And he is oblivious to his own construct aside from the objects that little girl begins to arrange and build. And the construct is stone, a hard surface, a door that allows no insect to enter. Outside the house, in the construct of America, tiny moths bash their brains into the aluminum siding. Woman watches them and thinks of no luxuries of dark rooms. No man and woman drifting. Little girl and little boy wailing and in need. The mail that arrives. The weather report. The dishes in the sink. Night, no luxury of language or sex. Time's imposition renders her weary and she dissolves from her own mind, behind the trees.

Woman is replica of obelisk. She wants to be obliterated by the dark and feels conspicuous by the light of morning. To be conspicuous is to be subject to scrutiny. Woman is not obelisk but America has made it necessary that she become one. Morning is man like obelisk calling all televisions into their routine and order. In the distance a door slams like the blink of a woman's eye, and little girl wakes and calls out into the mystery of existence. Bird jostles a bush and little boy is waking as though sleep was myth. In the myth of sleep man forgets that he is man. In the myth of sleep woman forgets that she is woman. In the morning she is not woman unless she is a quiet turmoil. She does not exist except in the turmoil of negation. Man bemoans his own entry into the construct and then begins running a machine. The machinery of daylight bemoans woman, who begins the turmoil of extension into obelisk. The obelisk is theory of obelisk and the machine ceases in its whir. The machine begins again, on and off, off and on, like the trajectory of daylight. Birds remain oblivious. Birds inform the template of daylight and of obelisk and of replica of obelisk, the absurd construct making man and woman certain and also full of doubt. The sweep of morning makes woman both hopeful and stagnant.

The rain submits to the silence prior to dusk. Little girl is holy and submits herself to the abeyance of rain. She babbles into the warm light of the kitchen. Woman feels the rain as a submission of her mind. Man is man to and fro and inconspicuous in his manhood. He says a word and then drifts from the room. Woman says a word and also drifts but is bulky like a train. There are things she intends to do which are good but she cannot bring herself to do them. She is distracted by the gray aura of rain and it makes her feel that she is consumed by rain; that the rain consumes all of woman, and the world is rain or woman. It reminds her of porches in the summertime, overcome with the hope of something lacking in stagnancy. Overcome with the orange glow of possibility. Without the specific coordinates. The big sky, inducing the hope of longevity. Woman reaches upward like an obelisk and then the obelisk dismantles itself. And she feels glad in this dismantling. She wants to be dismantled, in the hush of rain's aftermath.

Woman is a proverbial torch that sets the head of man aflame with passion and anger. She feels human life inside of her like a growing flame and begins to soften, become ingratiated to duty. Eventually it is duty which defines her and renders her woman. She beats the rug against the railing. She wanders around the marsh and attempts to find a hermetic self. She wants the indemnity of the self aside from the rule and duty of man. Man wants to set off walking or driving, swallow beer and look at the wooden faces of woman. It makes his heart feel as if the invigoration of the sea. It makes his heart feel unburned and unburdened, directionless and glad. It renders woman heavy with weeping, like a cloak. Woman commits to her duty and finds delight in the steady hum of a sewing machine. She feels child in her like a city at night. She feels child in her like a trespass. Along the marsh she feels owner-ship of something. When man goes astray his feels ownership of his own soul. At night they lie together unmoving and feel their respective ownerships. Sometimes, woman touches his cheek, just barely, and feels a dark passion, like a shadow slipping against his skin. The wind is in is the trees like a thousand insects ruling the earth. Insects rule the earth and this is not America, and it is.

In the late afternoon the sunlight is murderous in the clouds. They swell with it to the point of distention and murder. Time is the ultimate captor. Woman feels the enslavement of time and laments. She a feels a moment or two of nothing in an ephemera of wind and knows eternity, but then it suddenly slips like the wail of a child, the anger of man, the dependency of things. Then she is duty. She is figment of the construct of man. She is figment of earthly Kingdom. Time is captor and her heart is weary like an exhaustive utterance of words. She wants to sit for hours and dream herself out of the world's construct. She wants to sit for hours and watch the alterations of sunlight, have no duty or rule, be inconspicuous. She wants the flight of a city at a night, but also the child in her, like the flight of a city. When the child latches its mouth to her nipple she feels eternity, joy in the purest sense of things. She feels God and it is not the God of the construct of man. It is God like light, obliterating time. It is God circumventing all constructs. It is a prior God. Man enters, and feels duty and rule. Man enters, and feels the presence of woman, and feels bound, and so establishes the book.

Woman feels the drudgery of man like a heavy rope. At night he admits he is animal and she weakens. She feels she is the duty of a river. She snakes the sallow ground of him and submits. She becomes nothing. There is love in nothing, and a merging in the nothing. She feels merged and displaced and glad in her oblivion. Eventually she must have this, and breakfast simmering in the pan. Eventually she must have the clean sunlight of renewal. So she submits to man and becomes man and man becomes woman. In the dark it isn't easy to tell. Nobody says a word. Passion makes them the construct of bodies or not bodies at all. It makes them less than bodies, less than words. It makes them less than minds. It makes them current and event. It makes them electric and beyond earth, beyond God, like an arbitrary moon. It makes them chaos. And chaos ensues until it does not. Eventually they are again slave to the construct of man. They are duty and misery. The breakfast simmers but they have minds and they do not desire their own minds. Their minds are toward God but God is a fleeting idea. God enters and blesses their warm souls but then they are again enslaved by the construct. They shuffle papers, attend to the endless wail of the world.

The differential of soft flowers on the lilac bush has grown stagnant and enduring. Eight flowers the color of orchid skies are as point of reference for woman. If you look close they are scarcely breathing. They widen open like a woman in love, like eyes, unblinking for lack of sleep. The sun slowly sinks and leaves a residue of orangey light in the spaces between the trees. Man is an issue of quelling. Quelled rage, quelled towering, quelled heaviness of foot. Woman is rush of things, the elapsing of time like a slow murder. Little girl clings to her and remembers vaguely dwelling within her. There is general hush of man and woman, of man vs. woman, of man towering over and swallowing woman. Woman likewise does not swallow man. Woman allows man to remain quelled amid an exultation of words. Woman is point of reference for the soft flowers and sits among them. She is not beautiful but the world adopts the beauty it sees. There is an old broom propped against the railing. The woman is in relationship with the broom but the relationship seems insignificant. Woman is always in relation to a broom. On a broom or not, woman dreams that she is flying into flesh-colored sunset.

Things are broken everywhere. Tax brackets, screen windows, small plastic rocking horses. This is America and there is a subtle howling in the air. Little boy is disconsolate. He wails on the living room floor and begins to fathom his oncoming manhood. He is uncertain. He is not familiar with the weight of himself. He does not know the weight of the construct that he begins to enter, and he does not know that he is also the history of constructs. It has been established, his biology a determinant for all pursuant grief. He must assume himself. If he does not assume himself he is subject to the tyranny of other men. And he is not a towering. He squirms and wails and the world remains stagnant in its corruption. Police sirens herald the evening and they are not the sound of Polizia sirens, low in their wail, less than emergent. Woman is a lethargy. Her body labors and her mind grasps for the solitude of words. When she finally finds solitude, she must reconfigure her brain. She must imagine flying off into the flesh-colored sunset. She must again be not woman. She must again be not man. The flesh-colored sunset is not the construct, and she must find herself within this.

Man is the threshold of subsequent things. When he sits in the midst of a house the house is wild with man. Again man falls into slumber and dreams not of the infrastructures of the world. He dreams rather of sharks and sea and is afraid of the sharks and also feels himself a shark. The sharks are a great adventure and man awakens like a shark out of the sea. When woman passes through the room the air is wild with the spirit of sharks. Eventually as the day evolves the sharks become ghosts in the back of his mind. But he still conducts himself like a shark. And he is also a baseball field. He is a deserted baseball field in summer and the ghosts of a kind of exultation fill his spirit. A large butterfly poises itself against the screen on the porch. Woman fixes on its wings, opening and closing like her love, when she wills it. Man leaves the house to search for God. Woman fathoms God in the butterfly and it makes her sick with grief and gladness. The late afternoon is a buzz of sunlight and early cicadas. Woman feels her own wilting. She feels wilted like a faulty pen-stroke. And she is the wall and she is like a pen-stroke drifting through rooms. When man returns to the house he is shark rising from the sea.

The overwhelming existence of the soft flowers does not falter. Black flies circle the empty wine glasses, buzz around the rim in a pesky manner. The sound of chimes fills the afternoon but the afternoon does not hear them. Woman hears them and the distant whir of a corrupt nation. America is traffic but America is also people and the people are scared and friendly or unfriendly. And consequence is contingent upon the people. Man is consequence and woman is an aspiring exactitude. Woman wants to exact things. The exactitude of woman are what makes the consequence of man. Woman sits with her notebook and calculates exactitudes and the consequence of man. And the consequence of woman is contingent upon the consequence of man. Man is shark but sleeping. In his sleep he is in a sea infested with sharks. When woman sleeps she is in a nightmare infested with dark buildings. And still the existence of the soft flowers does not falter in the daylight. In the daylight woman attempts to harbor vitality. Vitality wanes and she clings to a tenuous faith.

The twitterpated birds move from tree to tree. Woman sees them and is envious that they are birds. She adopts the intellect of man but it is circumstantial and sublimated. She is the intellect of man with cunt to temper it. She is the intellect of man which must integrate and kill the construct. God is mother and mother of God is God and she reigns blindly. And the construct is blind to mother and mother-God. Mother God sees woman and man but cannot thwart the force of his construct. Among the construct is an infestation of buildings where woman sometimes enters and becomes man and becomes less than man in her manhood. Man enters buildings and is sometimes less than himself. The soft flowers are the antithesis of the infestation but man enjoys them anyway and they are on the wall of the buildings. There is a soft breeze titillating the trees. The chimes get swallowed by the afternoon sun and woman struggles to remain vital. Man sees woman and wants to possess her. He sees her mouth, dancing with language. He takes her to a dark place and cares not for his conscience. He sees her as willowy counterpart or as differential species. He forgets woman in his pursuit of woman and devours her, and kisses her, and leaves her in the solitude of darkness.

Woman resents the facility of her own sight. She'd rather her eyes were closed while she went on in a state of consciousness. She'd rather she did not see before her the weeds growing, reaching upward for lack of rule. She'd rather the sunlight were not so iridescent in her exhaustion. She tends to little girl and to little boy and again falls into the inundation of the sea. The sea is sleep and the sea of sleep is guilt and lost time. She does not want to lose time and time is a Father, man's arthritic hand curled and fighting against death. And she wants to come to terms with impending death. The exact lack of purpose of being born. Unless for resurrection and a freer self and soul. Man plays his piano at the threshold of dusk and the falling sunlight buzzes like the threshold of the sea of sleep. And woman wants to fall into the sea. Little girl and little boy are roused and eager to be away from the sea of sleep and woman feels her body drop with sleep. Man continues to play into the falling sun and woman feels the subtle wind like a prior time, prior to little girl and little boy, prior to the drudgery of Father time.

Woman feels the pull of life from another room in the house. Life is expectant and life is wanting and life is wanting to be fed and washed. The floors are needing to be swept. Everything needs to be washed: clothes, dishes, floors, little boy and little girl. Life is a washing of things. Life is the dull ache in the arms. Life is words, here and there, an occasional insight amid the washing. The air falls cooler and distant voices call into the falling sun. The blue jay persists. Man continues to play and play and he is a voice which fills the house and vibrates the walls. And the walls are filled with man. And the walls are filled with the intercourse of man and woman. They stand stalwart and tall and do not falter. Man enters the room and is distressed and disgruntled. He is dissatisfied with woman. Woman feels shame, like a shadow descended upon her and she does not know the difference between self and impending death. And she does not know the difference between self and the life that pulls at her, from the other room.

Emily Vogel's poetry, reviews, essays, and translations have most recently been published in *Omniverse, The Paterson Literary Review, Lips, City Lit Rag, Luna Luna, Maggy, Lyre Lyre, The Comstock Review, The Broome Review, Tiferet, The San Pedro River Review, 2 Bridges Review,* and *PEN,* among others. She is the author of five chapbooks, and two full-length collections: *The Philosopher's Wife* (Chester River Press, 2011) and *First Words* (NYQ Books, 2015); as well as, a collaborative book of poetry, *West of Home,* with her husband Joe Weil (Blast Press). She teaches writing at SUNY Oneonta and Hartwick College, and lives with her husband, the poet Joe Weil, and their two children, Clare and Gabriel.